Dream-Crowned
Traumgekrönt

Rainer Maria Rilke

Translated from the German
by
Lorne Mook

Printed in the United States of America

Rainer Maria Rilke

Traumgekrönt

ISBN: 978-1-60801-041-7

Library of Congress Control Number: 2010937170

University of New Orleans Press
unopress.org

Contents

Translator's Introduction

René Maria Rilke was celebrating his twenty-first birthday and already publishing his third book of poems: *Traumgekrönt (Dream-Crowned)*. It was December 1896. Three months had passed since he had moved from his birthplace of Prague to Munich. In five months more, he would meet an older woman named Lou Andreas-Salomé; they would become lovers, and at her urging he would change his name from René to Rainer. Rainer Maria Rilke would later write *The Book of Images, New Poems, Duino Elegies, Sonnets to Orpheus*, and much more, and would become the poet often named as the greatest in German (and among the greatest in any language) of the last century.

A decade has passed since the twenty-first century began; and yet, only now, in these pages, is that third book by Rilke translated into English. Given how highly he is esteemed and how widely he is read, and given the multiple English translations of so much of his other work, how can this be?

Rilke himself is partly to blame. He eventually dismissed this early work, and yet the dismissal is not unique or even particularly noteworthy: many writers look back on their early productions as if they were youthful indiscretions, and scholars and translators nevertheless remain interested. Nor, in Rilke's case, is the dismissal complete. His first book, *Leben und Lieder (Life and Songs)*, was never republished in his lifetime; but in 1913 he did approve the publication of *Erste Gedichte (First Poems)*, which collected the poems in *Traumgekrönt*—as well as those in the books that preceded and followed it: *Larenopfer (Offerings to Lares)* and *Advent*. Of course, Rilke is also partly to blame because his later work (so distinctively his own and yet so various and variously suggestive) offered plenty to keep translators occupied.

When first published in 1896, *Traumgekrönt* bore an epigraph from *Episoden* by Richard Zoozmann, the man who had helped fund the publication of Rilke's book:

> Pfadschaffend naht sich eine grosse
> Mit neuen Göttern schwangre Zeit.
>
> Path-creating, a great time
> pregnant with new gods approaches.

The poems in the book could hardly live up to such a grand statement, but many of them do represent something new in Rilke's work. If in his previous book, *Larenopfer,* Rilke often captures the soul of a space (namely Prague), in *Traumgekrönt* he often presents the space of the soul or, put differently, the drama of the soul in spatial terms. (For example, the soul swells until it is wrapped around the world's darkness, or happiness falls from heaven and hangs upon the soul like folded wings.) When I think about what makes many of Rilke's later poems distinctively Rilkean, this capacity for presenting the drama of the soul (and of the mind and heart as well) in spatial terms is what I think about most.

It is fitting that a book called *Dream-Crowned* should begin with a prefatory poem (written in September 1896, just before Rilke left Prague) called "King's Song." Since the poem is clearly addressed *to* a king, perhaps we are meant to imagine the king reassuring *himself* that he would remain a king even with no crown. (Given the book's title, perhaps an ability to dream is what will keep him kingly.) The rest of the book consists of two long sequences, each titled with an infinitive form of a verb. The twenty-eight poems of "To Dream" are very loosely connected by their concern with remembering or imagining or dreaming. Almost all were written (or at least completed) in Prague, mostly in the spring and summer of 1896; but numbers V, VIII, and XVII are from 1894, IV and XV from 1895. Numbers IX and XVI, both of which feature forests, were written in the wooded hills around Dittersbach, about sixty miles north of Prague, in July 1895. Numbers VI, XVIII, and XXI were completed in October 1896, just after Rilke's move to Munich. The twenty-two poems in "To Love" suggest the full trajectory of a romantic relationship. Written mostly between April and September of 1896, they cannot help but owe something to Rilke's own first long-term relationship—with Valerie (called Vally) von David-Rhônfeld. It had lasted over two years, with varying degrees of seriousness, before fading and then ending decisively with Rilke's farewell letter in December 1895.

Because Rilke wrote all of these poems in meter and rhyme (sometimes using almost-baroque rhyme schemes), and because not only the soul but also the body of a poem makes that poem what it is, I have imitated Rilke's meter and used rhyme (albeit often slant rhyme) wherever it has been possible to do so. One of a translator's laments is that such things are not possible as often as one would like. Take, for example, the case of rhyming lines that end on unaccented syllables, as in the German words *ertragen* and *sagen*. Occasionally, I have been able to preserve both rhyme and unaccented ending (as in *honor* and *brother*, or *ailing* and *straying*). More often, I have preserved one or the other. But there are many cases when even this was not possible without losing Rilke's meaning, and so the balance between body and soul tipped in soul's favor.

For any success these translations achieve, I am

grateful to Inge Fink, Shannon Pearson, Don Bogen, and Thom Satterlee, who read and studied them and offered extensive advice about how to improve them; and to the editors of *International Poetry Review*, *Poetry International*, and *Unsplendid*, who encouraged me by including them (or earlier versions of them) in their pages.

Dream-Crowned

Traumgekrönt

Königslied

Darfst das Leben mit Würde ertragen,
nur die Kleinlichen macht es klein;
Bettler können dir Bruder sagen,
und du kannst doch ein König sein.

Ob dir der Stirne göttliches Schweigen
auch kein rotgoldener Reif unterbrach,—
Kinder werden sich vor dir neigen,
selige Schwärmer staunen dir nach.

Tage weben aus leuchtender Sonne
dir deinen Purpur und Hermelin,
und, in den Händen Wehmut und Wonne,
liegen die Nächte vor dir auf den Knien . . .

King's Song

You shall bear this life with honor,
while the small-minded make it a small thing;
beggars could call you brother,
and still you would be a king.

If no red-gold circlet disrupted
the god-like silence of your brow,
blessed crowds would still be awestruck
and before you children would bow.

The days weave their purple and ermine
for you from the sunlight's strands,
and for you nights are down on their knees
with sadness and joy in their hands . . .

Träumen

I

Mein Herz gleicht der vergessenen Kapelle;
auf dem Altare prahlt ein wilder Mai.
Der Sturm, der übermütige Geselle,
brach längst die kleinen Fenster schon entzwei;
er schleicht herein jetzt bis zur Sakristei
und zerrt dort an der Ministrantenschelle.
Der schrillen Glocke zager Sehnsuchtsschrei
ruft zu der längst entwöhnten Opferstelle
den arg erstaunten fernen Gott herbei.
Da lacht der Wind und hüpft durchs Fenster frei.
Doch der Erzürnte packt des Klanges Welle
und schmettert an den Fliesen sie entzwei.

Und arme Wünsche knien in langer Reih
vorm Tor und betteln an vermooster Schwelle.
Doch längst schon geht kein Beter mehr vorbei.

To Dream

I

My heart resembles a forgotten chapel;
on the altar, showing off, is a wild May.
The tempest, his high-spirited companion,
shattered the small windows long ago;
now he creeps as far as the sacristy
where he tugs at the acolyte's altar bell.
The shrill bell's little timidly yearning cry
calls the very astonished, distant god
to the long-disused place of sacrifice.
The wind laughs there and leaps through the window, free.
But the Indignant seizes the sound wave
and on the tiles smashes it in two.

And abject wishes kneel in a long row
outside the gate and beg at the mossy threshold.
Time passes, but no worshipper passes through.

II

Ich denke an:

Ein Dörfchen schlicht in des Friedens Prangen,
drin Hahngekräh;
und dieses Dörfchen verloren gegangen
im Blütenschnee.

Und drin im Dörfchen mit Sonntagsmienen
ein kleines Haus;
ein Blondkopf nickt aus den Tüllgardinen
verstohlen heraus.

Rasch auf die Türe, die angelheiser
um Hilfe ruft,—
und dann in der Stube ein leiser, leiser
Lavendelduft . . .

II

I think of . . .

a tiny village simple in the splendor
of peace at cock-crow;
and this tiny village having been lost
in the blossom-snow.
And in the village, a little house
with a Sunday air;
from tulle curtains, a furtive nod—
a head with blonde hair.
Quickly at the door that calls for help
hoarse-hinged,—
and then the room with a faint, faint scent
of lavender tinged . . .

III

Mir ist: ein Häuschen wär mein eigen;
vor seiner Türe säß ich spät,
wenn hinter violetten Zweigen
bei halbverhalltem Grillengeigen
die rote Sonne sterben geht.

Wie eine Mütze grünlich-samten
steht meinem Haus das moosge Dach,
und seine kleinen, dickumrammten
und blankverbleiten Scheiben flammten
dem Tage heiße Grüße nach.

Ich träumte, und mein Auge langte
schon nach den blassen Sternen hin,—
vom Dorfe her ein Ave bangte,
und ein verlorner Falter schwankte
im schneeig schimmernden Jasmin.

Die müde Herde trollte trabend
vorbei, der kleine Hirte pfiff,—
und in die Hand das Haupt vergrabend,
empfand ich, wie der Feierabend
in meiner Seele Saiten griff.

III

Imagine . . . my own small house:
there's the door that I sit by
when, late, behind the violet branches,
to the crickets' half-muffled fiddling,
the red sun's lying down to die.

Much like a greenish-velvet cap,
my house's mossy roof looks smart,
and the small, thickly framed, and shiny
window panes flash their hot greetings
toward the day they see depart.

I dreamed, and already my eye
toward the pale stars reached out,—
an Ave trembled from the village,
and in the snowy, shimmering jasmine
a lost moth fluttered about.

The little shepherd whistled; the flock
tottered on its weary way,—
and burying my head in my hand
I felt how the strings of my very soul
were played upon by the close of day.

IV

Eine alte Weide trauert
dürr und fühllos in den Mai,—
eine alte Hütte kauert
grau und einsam hart dabei.

War ein Nest einst in der Weide,
in der Hütt ein Glück zu Haus;
Winter kam und Weh,—und beide
blieben aus . . .

IV

An old willow weeps
dead-hearted and dry in May;
nearby, an old hut droops,
grimly desolate and gray.

A nest was once in the willow,
good fortune at home in the hut;
and both—since winter came, and woe—
have stayed away . . .

V

Die Rose hier, die gelbe,
gab gestern mir der Knab,
heut trag ich sie, dieselbe,
hin auf sein frisches Grab.

An ihren Blättern lehnen
noch lichte Tröpfchen,—schau!
Nur heute sind es Tränen,—
und gestern war es Tau ...

V

Yesterday the boy
this rose, the yellow, gave—
the same I carry today
to place on his fresh grave.

Look! The leaves now lean
with droplets still in view.
Today they are the tears
that yesterday were dew . . .

VI

Wir saßen beisammen im Dämmerlichte.
»Mütterchen«, schmeichelte ich, »nicht wahr,
du erzählst mir noch einmal die schöne Geschichte
von der Prinzessin mit goldnem Haar?«—

Seit Mütterchen tot ist, durch dämmernde Tage
führt mich die Sehnsucht, die blasse Frau;
und von der schönen Prinzessin die Sage
weiß sie wie Mütterchen ganz genau ...

VI

We sat together in the twilight.
"Mamma," I coaxed, "as often you've told,
can you tell again the beautiful story
of the princess with hair of gold?"—

With Mamma dead, through twilights the yearning,
the pale woman, now leads me;
and like Mamma, she knows the saga
of the beautiful princess entirely . . .

VII

Ich wollt, sie hätten statt der Wiege
mir einen kleinen Sarg gemacht,
dann wär mir besser wohl, dann schwiege
die Lippe längst in feuchter Nacht.

Dann hätte nie ein wilder Wille
die bange Brust durchzittert,—dann
wärs in dem kleinen Körper stille,
so still, wie's niemand denken kann.

Nur eine Kinderseele stiege
zum Himmel hoch so sacht,—ganz sacht ...
Was haben sie mir statt der Wiege
nicht einen kleinen Sarg gemacht?—

VII

I wish they had, instead of a cradle,
made a little coffin for me.
That would be better for me. Then, the lip
would be long hushed in the damp night.

Then, never would have a wild will
trembled through the anxious breast.
The little body would then be still
with a stillness that can never be guessed.

Only a child-soul can climb
so softly, quite softly, to heaven's height . . .
Why have they not, instead of a cradle,
made a little coffin for me?—

VIII

Jene Wolke will ich neiden,
die dort oben schweben darf!
Wie sie auf besonnte Heiden
ihre schwarzen Schatten warf.

Wie die Sonne zu verdüstern
sie vermochte kühn genug,
wenn die Erde lichteslüstern
grollte unter ihrem Flug.

All die goldnen Strahlenfluten
jener Sonne wollt auch ich
hemmen! Wenn auch für Minuten!
Wolke! Ja, ich neide dich!

VIII

I will envy that cloud there
that can float overhead!
How onto sunlit heaths
it threw its black shade.

How it was daring enough
to darken the sun's light,
making the light-lusting earth
grumble under its flight.

I'd keep all the golden ray-floods
of that sun from passing through
if I could! If only for minutes!
Cloud! How I envy you!

IX

Mir ist: Die Welt, die laute, kranke,
hat jüngst zerstört ein jäh Zerstieben,
und mir nur ist der Weltgedanke,
der große, in der Brust geblieben.

Denn so ist sie, wie ich sie dachte;
ein jeder Zwiespalt ist vertost:
auf goldnen Sonnenflügeln sachte
umschwebt mich grüner Waldestrost.

IX

It seems . . . the world, the loud and ailing,
has just been destroyed, abruptly dispersed,
and only for me does the world-thought,
the large, remain within the breast.

Then it is as I have thought it;
each discord has played all its notes:
around me, gently, on golden sun-wings,
green comfort of the forest floats.

X

Wenn das Volk, das drohnenträge,
trabt den altvertrauten Trott,
möcht ich weiße Wandelwege
wallen durch das Duftgehege
ernst und einsam wie ein Gott.

Wandeln nach den glanzdurchsprühten
Fernen, lichten Lohns bewußt;—
um die Stirne kühle Blüten
und von kinderkeuschen Mythen
voll die sabbatstille Brust.

X

When the people who idly drone are treading
with old assurance the track they've trod,
I wish for a clean path to travel,
to move through fragrant places as solemn
and solitary as a god.

Knowing the bright rewards, to wander
distances where glory shines through spray;—
with cool blossoms around the forehead
and myths as chaste as children filling
a breast as still as the seventh day.

XI

Weiss ich denn, wie mir geschieht?
In den Lüften Düftequalmen
und in bronzebraunen Halmen
ein verlornes Grillenlied.

Auch in meiner Seele klingt
tief ein Klang, ein traurig-lieber,—
so hört wohl ein Kind im Fieber,
wie die tote Mutter singt.

XI

Do I know how my life moves along?
In the air, dense smoke of perfumes,
and in bronze-brown grasses
a forlorn cricket song.

Also in my soul there rings,
deeply, a sound sadly dear,—
as a child in the fever may hear
how the dead mother sings.

XII

Schon blinzt aus argzerfetztem Laken
der holde, keusche Götternacken
der früherwachenden Natur,
und nur in tiefentlegnen Talen
zeigt hinter violetten, kahlen
Gebüschen sich mit falschem Prahlen
des Winters weiße Sohlenspur.

Hin geh ich zwischen Weidenbäumen
an nassen Räderrinnensäumen
den Fahrweg, und der Wind ist mild.
Die Sonne prangt im Glast des Märzen
und zündet an im dunkeln Herzen
der Sehnsucht weiße Opferkerzen
vor meiner Hoffnung Gnadenbild.

XII

Already early-waking nature
shows through a sheet that's badly tattered
the lovely, chaste neck of a god;
and only in valleys deep and narrow,
behind some bare and violet bushes,
winter displays, with mistaken boasting,
a trace of white where it has trod.

Out I go between the willows
on wet wheel-ruts of the highway,
and the wind is mild. The sun's on fire
in the radiance of March and kindles
the white offertory candles
in front of my hope's sacred image
in the dark heart of my desire.

XIII

Fahlgrauer Himmel, von dem jede Farbe
bange verblich.
Weit—ein einziger lohroter Strich
wie eine brennende Geißelnarbe.

Irre Reflexe vergehn und erscheinen.
Und in der Luft
liegts wie ersterbender Rosenduft
und wie verhaltenes Weinen . . .

XIII

The ash-gray sky from which each color, fearful,
faded. And far—
a single blazing-red streak burning
like a whip-scar.

A crazy pattern of colors passes away
and reappears.
And lies in the air like dying rose-scent,
like held-back tears . . .

XIV

Die Nacht liegt duftschwer auf dem Parke,
und ihre Sterne schauen still,
wie schon des Mondes weiße Barke
im Lindenwipfel landen will.

Fern hör ich die Fontäne lallen
ein Märchen, das ich längst vergaß,—
und dann ein leises Apfelfallen
ins hohe, regungslose Gras.

Der Nachtwind schwebt vom nahen Hügel
und trägt durch alte Eichenreihn
auf seinem blauen Falterflügel
den schweren Duft vom jungen Wein.

XIV

The night, scent-heavy, lies on the park
and, quiet, her stars look out and see
how already the moon's white bark
wants to land in the top of the linden tree.

I hear in the distant fountain's babble
a long-forgotten fairy tale,—
and in the high, motionless grass
the faint sound of an apple-fall.

From the nearby hill, the night-wind floats
past old oaks planted in a line
and carries on his blue butterfly wing
the heavy scent of the young wine.

XV

Im Schooß der silberhellen Schneenacht
dort schlummert alles weit und breit,
und nur ein ewig wildes Weh wacht
in einer Seele Einsamkeit.

Du fragst, warum die Seele schwiege,
warum sie's in die Nacht hinaus
nicht gießt?—Sie weiß, wenns ihr entstiege,
es löschte alle Sterne aus.

XV

Far and wide, all things slumber
in the lap of the silvery night of snow;
but awake in one soul's isolation
is one everlasting wild woe.

You ask: why would the soul be silent,
why not pour forth into the night?—
She knows that if she comes out under
the stars, she will put out their light.

XVI

Abendläuten. Aus den Bergen hallt es
wieder neu zurück in immer mattern
Tönen. Und ein Lüftchen fühlst du flattern
von dem grünen Talgrund her, ein kaltes.

In den weißen Wiesenquellen lallt es
wie ein Stammeln kindischen Gebetes;
durch den schwarzen Tannenhochwald geht es
wie ein Dämmern, ein jahrhundertaltes.

Durch die Fuge eines Wolkenspaltes
wirft der Abend rote Blutkorallen
nach den Felsenwänden.—Und sie prallen
lautlos von den Schultern des Basaltes.

XVI

Evening bell. From the mountains it gets retold
in echoes whose tones grow more and more
subdued. And you feel, rising from the floor
of the green valley, a fluttering breeze, a cold one.

In the white meadow-springs, it babbles on
like stammering small children saying prayers;
through the black alpine forest thick with firs,
it passes like a twilight, a century-old one.

Through the gap that forms when one cloud is unrolled
from another, the evening casts a red display
of blood-corals at the rock walls.—They ricochet
inaudibly from off the basalt shoulders.

XVII

Weltenweiter Wandrer,
walle fort in Ruh . . .
also kennt kein andrer
Menschenleid wie du.

  Wenn mit lichtem Leuchten
du beginnst den Lauf,
schlägt der Schmerz die feuchten
Augen zu dir auf.

Drinnen liegt—als riefen
sie dir zu: Versteh!—
tief in ihren Tiefen
eine Welt voll Weh . . .

Tausend Tränen reden
ewig ungestillt,
und in einer jeden
spiegelt sich dein Bild!

XVII

World-wide wanderer,
in peace keep traveling . . .
no one knows like you do
human suffering.

When you begin upon
your course with a bright glow,
the pain opens its moist
eyes toward you.

Within their deepest depths
there lies—as if to you
they cried out: Understand!—
a world full of woe . . .

A thousand tears speak,
unappeased forever,
and in each you find
your image, as in a mirror!

XVIII

Möchte mir ein blondes Glück erkiesen;
doch vom Sehnen bin ich müd und Suchen.—
Weiße Wasser gehn in stillen Wiesen,
und der Abend blutet in die Buchen.

Mädchen wandern heimwärts. Rot im Mieder
Rosen; ferneher verklingt ihr Lachen . . .
Und die ersten Sterne kommen wieder
und die Träume, die so traurig machen.

XVIII

If a blonde fate should like to choose me ...
but I've grown weary of yearning and searching.—
White water runs in the quiet meadows,
and into the beeches evening's bleeding.

Girls walk homeward, the red of roses
in bodices; far off, their laughter
fades away ... And the first stars
come back—and the dreams that make one sadder.

XIX

Vor mir liegt ein Felsenmeer,
Sträucher, halb im Schutt versunken.
Todesschweigen.—Nebeltrunken
hangt der Himmel drüber her.

Nur ein matter Falter schwirrt
rastlos durch das Land, das kranke ...
Einsam, wie ein Gottgedanke
durch die Brust des Leugners irrt.

XIX

Before me lies a rock-sea.
Shrubs, in the debris half-sunk,
deathly quiet.—Mist-drunk
above it hangs the sky.

Only a moth, a feeble flier,
whirs restless through the land, the ailing . . .
Lonely, like a God-thought straying
through the breast of a denier.

XX

Die Fenster glühten an dem stillen Haus,
der ganze Garten war voll Rosendüften.
Hoch spannte über weißen Wolkenklüften
der Abend in den unbewegten Lüften
die Schwingen aus.

Ein Glockenton ergoß sich auf die Au ...
Lind wie ein Ruf aus himmlischen Bezirken.
Und heimlich über flüstervollen Birken
sah ich die Nacht die ersten Sterne wirken
ins blasse Blau.

XX

The bright windows glowed in the silent house;
the whole garden was full of the scent of roses.
High in the sky, above the white cloud-chasms,
the evening stretched its pinions in the air
now motionless.

The bell sounds poured themselves onto the lea ...
Mild as a call from out of heavenly districts.
And secretly over birches full of whispers
I saw the first stars of the night appearing
in the pale blue.

XXI

Es gibt so wunderweiße Nächte,
drin alle Dinge Silber sind.
Da schimmert mancher Stern so lind,
als ob er fromme Hirten brächte
zu einem neuen Jesuskind.

Weit wie mit dichtem Demantstaube
bestreut, erscheinen Flur und Flut,
und in die Herzen, traumgemut,
steigt ein kapellenloser Glaube,
der leise seine Wunder tut.

XXI

There are the clear nights of wonder
in which all things are silver.
Many a star gleams as mild
as though bringing devout shepherds
to a new Christ Child.

Broad field and flood seem powdered
with a thick dust of diamonds,
and there's a faith without chapels,
in hearts that are dream-feeling,
that quietly works its miracles.

XXII

Wie eine Riesenwunderblume prangt
voll Duft die Welt, an deren Blütenspelze,
ein Schmetterling mit blauem Schwingenschmelze,
die Mainacht hangt.

Nichts regt sich; nur der Silberfühler blinkt . . .
Dann trägt sein Flügel ihn, sein frühverblaßter,
nach Morgen, wo aus feuerroter Aster
er Sterben trinkt . . .

XXII

Like a giant miracle-flower, the world is bright
and full of fragrance; in its blossom-fur,
like a butterfly with blue glaze on its wings
hangs the May night.

Nothing stirs; only the silver feeler blinks . . .
His early-fading wing then carries him
toward morning, where from an aster, fire-red,
his death he drinks . . .

XXIII

Wie, jegliches Gefühl vertiefend,
ein süßer Drang die Brust bewegt,
wenn sich die Mainacht, sternetriefend,
auf mäuschenstille Plätze legt.

Da schleichst du hin auf sachter Sohle
und schwärmst zum blanken Blau hinauf,
und groß wie eine Nachtviole
geht dir die dunkle Seele auf ...

XXIII

How, every feeling growing deeper,
a sweet urging moves the breast
when the May night, its stars dripping,
in mouse-still places finds its rest.

You sneak there on soft soles and raise
adoring eyes to the clear blue,
and large like a dame's violet
your dark soul opens up in you.

XXIV

O gäbs doch Sterne, die nicht bleichen,
wenn schon der Tag den Ost besäumt;
von solchen Sternen ohnegleichen
hat meine Seele oft geträumt.

Von Sternen, die so milde blinken,
daß dort das Auge landen mag,
das müde ward vom Sonnetrinken
an einem goldnen Sommertag.

Und schlichen hoch ins Weltgetriebe
sich wirklich solche Sterne ein,—
sie müßten der verborgnen Liebe
und allen Dichtern heilig sein.

XXIV

When day already edges the east,
O still give the never-fading star;
my soul has often dreamed of just
such stars as this without compare.

Of stars that go on twinkling
so mildly that there the eye
may land when tired from sun-drinking
on a golden summer day.

And if, high up, such stars could really
slip into what makes the world move,
then to all poets they'd be holy—
just as they are to hidden love.

XXV

Mir ist so weh, so weh, als müßte
die ganze Welt in Grau vergehn,
als ob mich die Geliebte küßte
und spräch: Auf Nimmerwiedersehn.

Als ob ich tot wär und im Hirne
mir dennoch wühlte wilde Qual,
weil mir vom Hügel eine Dirne
die letzte, blasse Rose stahl . . .

XXV

It seems that the whole world must cease
in gray, I feel such pain, such pain—
as if the beloved kissed me and said:
We'll never see each other again.

As if I were dead and in the brain
a wild torment tunneled still,
because there was a wench who stole
the last, pale rose from my hill . . .

XXVI

Matt durch der Tale Gequalme wankt
Abend auf goldenen Schuhn,—
Falter, der träumend am Halme hangt,
weiß nichts vor Wonne zu tun.

   Alles schlürft heil an der Stille sich.—
Wie da die Seele sich schwellt,
daß sie als schimmernde Hülle sich
legt um das Dunkel der Welt.

XXVI

Faintly through smoking valleys the evening
totters on golden shoes;
moth, which hangs on the stalk dreaming,
knows not what to do with its joys.

All things sip their health at the stillness.—
So much does the soul swell
that around the darkness of the world
it forms a shimmering shell.

XXVII

Ein Erinnern, das ich heilig heiße,
leuchtet mir durchs innerste Gemüt,
so wie Götterbildermarmorweiße
durch geweihter Haine Dämmer glüht.

Das Erinnern einstger Seligkeiten,
das Erinnern an den toten Mai,—
Weihrauch in den weißen Händen, schreiten
meine stillen Tage dran vorbei ...

XXVII

Through the innermost mind, a memory
that I call holy shines me its light,
as through the dusk of sacred groves
the forms of marble gods glow white.

The memory of blessings past,
the memory of the dead May,—
with incense in their white hands, there
my silent days go striding by . . .

XXVIII

Glaubt mir, daß ich, matt vom Kranken,
keinen lauten Lenz mehr mag,—
will nur einen sonnenblanken,
wipfelroten Frühherbsttag.

Will die Lust, die jubelschrille,
nicht mehr in die Brust zurück,—
will nur Sterbestubenstille
drinnen—für mein totes Glück.

XXVIII

Believe me: weary of all ailing,
I'd like no more loud springtime fray;
want only a sunny, brightly shining,
treetop-red early autumn day.

I want no more the youthful desire,
the jubilant-shrill, back in my breast;
want only death-room silence inside—
where my dead happiness can rest.

Lieben

I

Und wie mag die Liebe dir kommen sein?
Kam sie wie ein Sonnen, ein Blütenschnein,
kam sie wie ein Beten?—Erzähle:

Ein Glück löste leuchtend aus Himmeln sich los
und hing mit gefalteten Schwingen groß
an meiner blühenden Seele . . .

To Love

I

And how might the love have come to you?
Came it like a sunning, a blossom-snow?
Came it like a praying?—Tell:

A happiness, among the heavenly things,
broke free and hung, grandly, with folded wings
upon my blossoming soul ...

II

Das war der Tag der weißen Chrysanthemen,—
mir bangte fast vor seiner schweren Pracht ...
Und dann, dann kamst du mir die Seele nehmen
tief in der Nacht.

Mir war so bang, und du kamst lieb und leise,—
ich hatte grad im Traum an dich gedacht.
Du kamst, und leis wie eine Märchenweise
erklang die Nacht ...

II

That was the day of the white chrysanthemums;
before their heavy splendor, I nearly took fright . . .
And then, then you came to take my soul
deep in the night.

I was afraid—and lovingly, softly, you came;
of you, within the dream, I had just thought.
You came, and softly like a fairy tune
the night rang out . . .

III

Einen Maitag mit dir beisammen sein,
und selbander verloren ziehn
durch der Blüten duftqualmende Flammenreihn
zu der Laube von weißem Jasmin.

Und von dorten hinaus in den Maiblust schaun,
jeder Wunsch in der Seele so still ...
Und ein Glück sich mitten in Mailust baun,
ein großes,—das ists, was ich will ...

III

To be together with you on a day in May
and, through the fragrant haze of flowers
in flaming rows, to wander aimlessly
to the white jasmine bower.

   And from there to gaze out at the May blossoms,
each wish within the soul made silent . . .
And to build in the middle of May-desire a great
happiness,—that's what I want . . .

IV

Ich weiß nicht, wie mir geschieht . . .
Weiß nicht, was Wonne ich lausche,
mein Herz ist fort wie im Rausche,
und die Sehnsucht ist wie ein Lied.

Und mein Mädel hat fröhliches Blut
und hat das Haar voller Sonne
und die Augen von der Madonne,
die heute noch Wunder tut.

IV

I don't know how this happened to me ...
don't know what joy I listen to;
my heart is away as in drunkenness,
and the longing is like a melody.

And my girl has a heart that's cheerful,
and hair that's full of sun,
and eyes of the Madonna,
who still today works miracles.

V

Ob du's noch denkst, daß ich dir Äpfel brachte
und dir das Goldhaar glattstrich leis und lind?
Weißt du, das war, als ich noch gerne lachte,
und du warst damals noch ein Kind.

Dann ward ich ernst. In meinem Herzen brannte
ein junges Hoffen und ein alter Gram . . .
Zur Zeit, als einmal dir die Gouvernante
den »Werther« aus den Händen nahm.

Der Frühling rief. Ich küßte dir die Wangen,
dein Auge sah mich groß und selig an.
Das war ein Sonntag. Ferne Glocken klangen,
und Lichter gingen durch den Tann . . .

V

Do you still remember that I brought you apples
and softly, gently smoothed your hair of gold?
You know . . . that was when I still liked to laugh,
and you were still a child.

Then I turned serious. Within my heart
a youthful hope and an old sorrow burned . . .
It was around that time the governess took
the *Werther* from out of your hand.

The spring cried out. I kissed your cheeks; your eye
looked upon me large and full of blessing.
That was a Sunday. Far off, bells rang, and through
the firs the lights were passing . . .

VI

Wir saßen beide in Gedanken
im Weinblattdämmer—du und ich—
und über uns in duftgen Ranken
versummte wo ein Hummel sich.

Reflexe hielten, bunte Kreise,
in deinem Haare flüchtig Rast . . .
Ich sagte nichts als einmal leise:
»Was du für schöne Augen hast.«

VI

We sat in thought, in the grape-leaf twilight,
together—you and I;
above us, in the scented tendrils,
was a buzzing bumblebee.

In your hair, many-colored patterns of circles
retained a brief repose . . .
I said nothing but, once and softly,
"You have such beautiful eyes."

VII

Blondköpfchen hinter den Scheiben
hebt es sich ab so fein,—
sternt es ins Stäubchentreiben
oder zu mir herein?

Ist es das Köpfchen, das liebe,
das mich gefesselt hält,
oder das Stäubchengetriebe
dort in der sonnigen Welt?

Keins sieht zum andern hinüber.
Heimlich, die Stirne voll Ruh
schreitet der Abend vorüber ...
Und wir? Wir sehn ihm halt zu.—

VII

Little blonde head beyond the panes
looks up with such delicacy,—
does she look, starry-eyed, at the swirling dust motes
or into my window at me?

Is it the little head, the loved,
that keeps me bound,
or is it the swirling dust motes there
in the sunny world?

Neither one sees the other.
In secret, with brow full of peace,
the evening strides on by . . .
And we? We just watch him pass.—

VIII

Die Liese wird heute just sechzehn Jahr.
Sie findet im Klee einen Vierling ...
Fern drängt sichs wie eine Bubenschar:
die Löwenzähne mit blondem Haar
betreut vom sternigen Schierling.

Dort hockt hinterm Schierling der Riesenpan,
der strotzige, lose Geselle.
Jetzt sieht er verstohlen die Liese nahn
und lacht und wälzt durch den Wiesenplan
des Windes wallende Welle ...

VIII

Liese turns sixteen today.
She finds a four-leaf among the clover . . .
Far off, in a swarm, like a bunch of boys,
the dandelions with blonde hair
are tended by the starry hemlock.

Behind the hemlock the giant Pan
crouches, that puffed-up, licentious fellow.
Now in secret he sees Liese near
and laughs and rolls the pulsing wave
of the wind through the open meadow . . .

IX

Ich träume tief im Weingerank
mit meiner blonden Kleinen;
es bebt ihr Händchen, elfenschlank,
im heißen Zwang der meinen.

So wie ein gelbes Eichhorn huscht
das Licht hin im Reflexe,
und violetter Schatten tuscht
ins weiße Kleid ihr Kleckse.

In unsrer Brust liegt glückverschneit
goldsonniges Verstummen.
Da kommt in seinem Sammetkleid
ein Hummel Segen summen . . .

IX

With my fair-haired little one I deeply
dream in the creeping vine;
her little hand, elf-slender, trembles
in the hot force of mine.

In the vine-made patterns, the light (much like
a yellow squirrel) flits,
and on her white frock the violet shadows
hand-paint their blots.

Silence lies sunny-golden
within our breast snow-bound in bliss.
In his velvet frock, a bumblebee
comes buzzing blessing to us . . .

X

Es ist ein Weltmeer voller Lichte,
das der Geliebten Aug umschließt,
wenn von der Flut der Traumgesichte
die keusche Seele überfließt.

Dann beb ich vor der Wucht des Schimmers
so wie ein Kind, das stockt im Lauf,
geht vor der Pracht des Christbaumzimmers
die Flügeltüre lautlos auf.

X

It is an ocean full of light
that the eyes of lovers enclose
when from the flood of the dream-vision
the chaste soul overflows.

It's then, before that shimmering's force,
I tremble—as a child on the way
through folding doors to the Christmas-tree room
stops hushed before the display.

XI

Ich war noch ein Knabe. Ich weiß, es hieß:
Heut kommt Base Olga zu Gaste.
Dann sah ich dich nahn auf dem schimmernden Kies,
ins Kleidchen gepreßt, ins verblaßte.

Bei Tisch saß man später nach Ordnung und Rang
und frischte sich mäßig die Kehle;
und wie mein Glas an das deine klang,
da ging mir ein Riß durch die Seele.

Ich sah dir erstaunt ins Gesicht und vergaß
mich dem Plaudern der andern zu einen,
denn tief im trockenen Halse saß
mir würgend ein wimmerndes Weinen.

Wir gingen im Parke.—Du sprachst vom Glück
und küßtest die Lippen mir lange,
und ich gab dir fiebernde Küsse zurück
auf die Stirne, den Mund und die Wange.

Und da machtest du leise die Augen zu,
die Wonne blind zu ergründen ...
Und mir ahnte im Herzen: da wärest du
am liebsten gestorben in Sünden ...

XI

I still was a boy. I know they said: Today
Cousin Olga will be our guest.
Then I saw you nearby on the shimmering gravel,
squeezed into the faded dress.

Later, at the table, by order and rank,
all cooled their throats moderately;
and as my glass rang on yours, a rip
tore through the soul of me.

I saw the surprise in your face and forgot
the others and their chat,
then choking a whimpering cry
deep in the dry throat I sat.

We walked in the park.—You kissed my lips long
and spoke of happiness,
and on the brow, the mouth, the cheek,
I returned each feverish kiss.

And there you softly closed your eyes,
the blind joy to discern . . .
And I surmised in my heart: you'd like
best of all to die there in sin . . .

XII

Die Nacht im Silberfunkenkleid
streut Träume eine Handvoll,
die füllen mir mit Trunkenheit
die tiefe Seele randvoll.

Wie Kinder eine Weihnacht sehn
voll Glanz und goldnen Nüssen,—
seh ich dich durch die Mainacht gehn
und alle Blumen küssen.

XII

The night in its sparkling silver dress
scatters dreams by the handful;
they fill me up with drunkenness
and my deep soul is brim-full.

As children yearn for a Christmas bright
with golden nuts and splendors,—
I see you go through this May night
and kiss all of the flowers.

XIII

Schon starb der Tag. Der Wald war zauberhaft,
und unter Farren bluteten Zyklamen,
die hohen Tannen glühten, Schaft bei Schaft,
es war ein Wind,—und schwere Düfte kamen.
Du warst von unserm weiten Weg erschlafft,
ich sagte leise deinen süßen Namen:
Da bohrte sich mit wonnewilder Kraft
aus deines Herzens weißem Liliensamen
die Feuerlilie der Leidenschaft.

Rot war der Abend—und dein Mund so rot,
wie meine Lippen sehnsuchtheiß ihn fanden,
und jene Flamme, die uns jäh durchloht,
sie leckte an den neidischen Gewanden ...
Der Wald war stille, und der Tag war tot.
Uns aber war der Heiland auferstanden,
und mit dem Tage starben Neid und Not.
Der Mond kam groß an unsern Hügeln landen,
und leise stieg das Glück aus weißem Boot.

XIII

Already the day died. The cyclamens bled
beneath the ferns in the enchanted forest
where, shaft by shaft, the high firs glowed;
there was a wind—and heavy fragrance.
From our long journey, you had grown tired;
I spoke your sweet name softly: there, with power
that was joy-wild, as though piercing the sod
the fire-lily of passion
sprang from your heart's white lily-seed.

Red was the evening—and your mouth so red,
as my lips hotly yearning discovered it,
and those flames that through us so quickly flared
licked the envious garments . . .
The forest was silent, and the day was dead.
To us, though, was the Savior risen,
and with the day died envy and need.
The moon came large to land on our hills and softly
the happiness rose from the white boat's bed.

XIV

Es leuchteten im Garten die Syringen,
von einem Ave war der Abend voll,—
da war es, daß wir voneinander gingen
in Gram und Groll.

Die Sonne war in heißen Fieberträumen
gestorben hinter grauen Hängen weit,
und jetzt verglomm auch hinter Blütenbäumen
dein weißes Kleid.

Ich sah den Schimmer nach und nach vergehen
und bangte bebend wie ein furchtsam Kind,
das lange in ein helles Licht gesehen:
Bin ich jetzt blind?—

XIV

The syringas made the garden glow;
of an Ave was the evening full,—
there it was that we left each other
in resentment and sorrow.

Far behind gray slopes, in the heat
of fever-dreams, the sun had died;
now your white dress behind flowering trees
had also gone out.

Afraid, seeing how the luster waned,
I trembled like a timorous child
that long has seen in a bright light:
Am I now blind?—

XV

Oft scheinst du mir ein Kind, ein kleines,—
dann fühl ich mich so ernst und alt,—
wenn nur ganz leis dein glockenreines
Gelächter in mir widerhallt.

Wenn dann in großem Kinderstaunen
dein Auge aufgeht, tief und heiß,—
möcht ich dich küssen und dir raunen
die schönsten Märchen, die ich weiß.

XV

Often you seem like a child, a small one,—
then how earnest and old I feel!—
All it takes is for your laughter
to resound in me pure as a bell.

If then, your eyes, deep and hot,
should open wide with child-like awe,
I'll want to kiss you and whisper to you
the loveliest fairy tales I know.

XVI

Nach einem Glück ist meine Seele lüstern,
nach einem kurzen, dummen Wunderwahn . . .
Im Quellenquirlen und im Föhrenflüstern
da hör ichs nahn . . .

Und wenn von Hügeln, die sich purpurn säumen,
in bleiche Bläue schwimmt der Silberkahn,—
dann unter schattenschweren Blütenbäumen
seh ich es nahn.

In weißem Kleid; so wie das Lieb, das tote,
am Sonntag mit mir ging durch Staub und Strauch,
am Herzen jene Blume nur, die rote,
trug es die auch? . . .

XVI

My soul lusts for a happiness,
for a brief, foolish madness of wonder . . .
There, in the spring's water-whirl and Scotch pines' whisper,
I hear it draw nearer . . .

And if the silver boat in pale blue swims
from the hills that are outlined with a purple border,—
then under the flowering trees heavy with shade
I see it draw nearer.

In a white dress; so like that love, the dead,
that went through dust and shrub with me on Sunday,
did it also wear upon the heart exactly
that flower, the red? . . .

XVII

Wir gingen unter herbstlich bunten Buchen,
vom Abschiedsweh die Augen beide rot ...
»Mein Liebling, komm, wir wollen Blumen suchen.«
Ich sagte bang: »Die sind schon tot.«

Mein Wort war lauter Weinen.—In den Äthern
stand kindisch lächelnd schon ein blasser Stern.
Der matte Tag ging sterbend zu den Vätern,
und eine Dohle schrie von fern.—

XVII

We walked beneath the bright autumnal beeches,
from sorrow of parting the eyes of both of us red . . .
"My darling, come, we'll go and look for flowers."
I answered, frightened: "They're already dead."

My word was loud weeping.—In the ethers
already childishly smiling was a pale star.
The languid day went dying to the fathers,
and a jackdaw cried from afar.—

XVIII

Im Frühling oder im Traume
bin ich dir begegnet einst,
und jetzt gehn wir zusamm durch den Herbsttag,
und du drückst mir die Hand und weinst.

Weinst du ob der jagenden Wolken?
Ob der blutroten Blätter? Kaum.
Ich fühl es: du warst einmal glücklich
im Frühling oder im Traum . . .

XVIII

In spring or in a dream
I met you long ago,
and now, together, we go through the autumn day,
and you squeeze my hand and cry.

Do you cry over the chasing clouds?
Over the blood-red leaves? Hardly.
I feel it: once you were happy
in spring or in a dream ...

XIX

Sie hatte keinerlei Geschichte,
ereignislos ging Jahr um Jahr—
auf einmal kams mit lauter Lichte . . .
die Liebe oder was das war.

Dann plötzlich sah sie's bang zerrinnen,
da liegt ein Teich vor ihrem Haus . . .
So wie ein Traum scheints zu beginnen,
und wie ein Schicksal geht es aus.

XIX

She had no history at all;
uneventfully went the years—
at once, it came with a pure light . . .
love, or whatever it was.

Then she watched it all dissolve
and become like a pond before her house . . .
So like a dream it seems to come,
and like a destiny it goes.

XX

Man merkte: der Herbst kam. Der Tag war schnell
erstorben im eigenen Blute.
Im Zwielicht nur glimmte die Blume noch grell
auf der Kleinen verbogenem Hute.

Mit ihrem zerschlissenen Handschuh strich
sie die Hand mir schmeichelnd und leise.—
Kein Mensch in der Gasse als sie und ich ...
Und sie bangte: Du reisest? »Ich reise.«

Da stand sie, das Köpfchen voll Abschiedsnot
in den Stoff meines Mantels vergrabend ...
Vom Hütchen nickte die Rose rot,
und es lächelte müde der Abend.

XX

One noticed: autumn came. The day was quickly
dying in its own blood.
In the twilight the flower on the little one's bent hat
was all that still dazzlingly glowed.

With her worn-out glove, my hand
she fawningly, softly caressed.—
No one in the lane but she and I . . .
And she worried: Must you go? "I must."

She stood there, burying in my coat's fabric
her head with farewell-distress filled . . .
On the little hat the red rose nodded
and the evening sleepily smiled.

XXI

Manchmal da ist mir: Nach Gram und Müh
will mich das Schicksal noch segnen,
wenn mir in feiernder Sonntagsfrüh
lachende Mädchen begegnen . . .
Lachen hör ich sie gerne.

Lange dann liegt mir das Lachen im Ohr,
nie kann ichs, wähn ich, vergessen . . .
Wenn sich der Tag hinterm Hange verlor,
will ich mirs singen . . . Indessen
singens schon oben die Sterne . . .

XXI

Sometimes it seems that destiny still wants
to bless me after trouble and grief
when I cross the path of laughing girls
(I like to hear them laugh)
early on a reverent Sunday.

Long after, their laughing lingers in my ear—
I can never, I think, forget . . .
When the day is lost behind the slope,
I want to sing it to myself . . . and yet
the stars sing it overhead already . . .

XXII

Es ist lang,—es ist lang . . .
wann—weiß ich gar nimmer zu sagen . . .
eine Glocke klang, eine Lerche sang—
und ein Herz hat so selig geschlagen.
Der Himmel so blank überm Jungwaldhang,
der Flieder hat Blüten getragen,—
und im Sonntagskleide ein Mädchen, schlank,
das Auge voll staunender Fragen . . .
Es ist lang,—es ist lang . . .

XXII

It's been long,—it's been long . . .
when—I cannot rightly say . . .
a bell rang, a lark sang—
and a heart was beating blessedly.
The sky so clear above the young
woods-slope, the lilac bore blossoms,—
and in Sunday dress a girl, thin,
eyes full of astonishing questions . . .
It's been long,—it's been long . . .

Also Available from **UNOPRESS**:

William Christenberry: Art & Family by J. Richard Gruber (2000)

The El Cholo Feeling Passes by Fredrick Barton (2003)

A House Divided by Fredrick Barton (2003)

Coming Out the Door for the Ninth Ward edited by Rachel Breunlinfrom from The Neighborhood Story Project series (2006)

The Change Cycle Handbook by Will Lannes (2008)

Cornerstones: Celebrating the Everyday Monuments & Gathering Places of New Orleans edited by Rachel Breunlin, from The Neighborhood Story Project series (2008)

A Gallery of Ghosts by John Gery (2008)

Hearing Your Story: Songs of History and Life for Sand Roses by Nabile Farès translated by Peter Thompson, from The Engaged Writers Series (2008)

The Imagist Poem: Modern Poetry in Miniature edited by William Pratt from The Ezra Pound Center for Literature series (2008)

The Katrina Papers: A Journal of Trauma and Recovery by Jerry W. Ward, Jr. from The Engaged Writers Series (2008)

On Higher Ground: The University of New Orleans at Fifty by Dr. Robert Dupont (2008)

Us Four Plus Four: Eight Russian Poets Conversing translated by Don Mager (2008)

Voices Rising: Stories from the Katrina Narrative Project edited by Rebeca Antoine (2008)

Gravestones (Lápidas) by Antonio Gamoneda, translated by Donald Wellman from The Engaged Writers Series (2009)

The House of Dance and Feathers: A Museum by Ronald W. Lewis by Rachel Breunlin & Ronald W. Lewis, from The Neighborhood Story Project series (2009)

I hope it's not over, and good-by: Selected Poems of Everette Maddox by Everette Maddox (2009)

Portraits: Photographs in New Orleans 1998-2009 by Jonathan Traviesa (2009)

Theoretical Killings: Essays & Accidents by Steven Church (2009)

Voices Rising II: More Stories from the Katrina Narrative Project edited by Rebeca Antoine (2010)

Rowing to Sweden: Essays on Faith, Love, Politics, and Movies by Fredrick Barton (2010)

Dogs in My Life: The New Orleans Photographs of John Tibule Mendes (2010)

Understanding the Music Business: A Comprehensive View edited by Harmon Greenblatt & Irwin Steinberg (2010)

The Fox's Window by Naoko Awa, translated by Toshiya Kamei (2010)

A Passenger from the West by Nabile Farès, translated by Peter Thompson from The Engaged Writers Series (2010)

The Schüssel Era in Austria: Contemporary Austrian Studies, Volume 18 edited by Günter Bischof & Fritz Plasser (2010)

The Gravedigger by Rob Magnuson Smith (2010)

Everybody Knows What Time It Is by Reginald Martin (2010)

When the Water Came: Evacuees of Hurricane Katrina by Cynthia Hogue & Rebecca Ross from The Engaged Writers Series (2010)

Aunt Alice Vs. Bob Marley by Kareem Kennedy, from The Neighborhood Story Project series (2010)

Houses of Beauty: From Englishtown to the Seventh Ward by Susan Henry from The Neighborhood Story Project series (2010)

Signed, The President by Kenneth Phillips, from The Neighborhood Story Project series (2010)

Beyond the Bricks by Daron Crawford & Pernell Russell from The Neighborhood Story Project series (2010)

Green Fields: Crime, Punishment, & a Boyhood Between by Bob Cowser, Jr., from the Engaged Writers Series (2010)

New Orleans: The Underground Guide by Michael Patrick Welch & Alison Fensterstock (2010)

Writer in Residence: Memoir of a Literary Translater by Mark Spitzer (2010)

Open Correspondence: An Epistolary Dialogue by Abdelkébir Khatibi and Rita El Khayat, translated by Safoi Babana-Hampton, Valérie K. Orlando, Mary Vogl from The Engaged Writers Series (2010)

Black Santa by Jamie Bernstein (2010)

From Empire to Republic: Post-World-War-I Austria: Contemporary Austrian Studies, Volume 19 edited by Günter Bischof, Fritz Plasser and Peter Berger (2010)

Vegetal Sex (O Sexo Vegetal) by Sergio Medeiros, translated by Raymond L.Bianchi (2010)

Dream-Crowned (Traumgekrönt) by Rainer Maria Rilke, translated by Lorne Mook (2010)

Wounded Days (Los Días Heridos) by Leticia Luna, translated by Toshiya Kamei (2010) from The Engaged Writers Series (2010)